ECONOMIC RECESSION 101: HOW TO PROTECT YOUR FINANCES

"Surviving Financial Turmoil: A Guide To Staying Afloat"

Emmanuel Akinnodi

substitute for professional advice. the author and publisher make no representations or warranties of any kind, express or implied, about the completeness, accuracy, reliability, suitability or availability with respect to the book or the information, products, services, or related graphics contained in the book for any purpose. any reliance you place on such information is therefore strictly at your own risk.

The author and publisher disclaim any liability or loss in connection with the content of this book.

Table of contents

INTRODUCTION

CHAPTER ONE

Understanding economic recessions
The impact of economic recessions on finances

CHAPTER TWO

Preparing for economic uncertainty
Building an emergency fund
Assessing your financial risk
Developing a budget

CHAPTER SIX

CHAPTER SEVEN

CONCLUSION

INTRODUCTION

Economic recessions are a fact of life. They are a natural part of the economic cycle, but they can have a devastating impact on individuals and businesses alike. The loss of jobs, decline in housing prices, and decline in consumer spending all contribute to a decline in the economy. The effects of a recession can be felt by nearly everyone, and it can take years for an economy to fully recover. But understanding what causes a recession, how to prepare for one and how to navigate the uncertainty can help us to mitigate the risks and come out stronger on the other side. this book aims to provide you with a comprehensive understanding of economic and the tools you need to protect your finances and build resilience in the face of economic uncertainty.

This book will cover the causes and triggers of economic recessions, the impact on finances, preparing for economic uncertainty, managing debt, protecting your career and income, support systems and government assistance, and strategies for moving forward after a recession. With the information and strategies provided in this book, you'll be able to navigate the economic downturn and come out on the other side with your finances intact. together, we'll explore the economic cycle, the causes and consequences of recessions, and most importantly, the steps you can take to protect yourself and your loved ones during these challenging times.

CHAPTER ONE
Understanding Economic Recessions

Economic recessions are a normal part of the business cycle, characterized by a decline in economic activity, employment, and trade. A recession is typically defined as two consecutive quarters of negative GDP growth, but it can also be identified by a decline in other economic indicators such as employment, industrial production, and retail sales.

Recessions can have a significant impact on the economy and society, leading to job losses, lower income and wealth, and reduced access to credit. Businesses may reduce production and lay off workers, leading to higher unemployment, and consumers may reduce spending, leading to a decline in consumer demand. This decline in demand can further exacerbate the recession, as businesses may reduce production further and lay off more workers.

There are various factors that can cause recession. One common cause is monetary policy, which refers to the actions of a country's central bank to control the money supply and interest rates. if the central bank raises interest rates too high, it can lead to a decline in borrowing and spending, which can cause a recession. Another cause can be government spending. If the government suddenly reduces its spending, it can lead to a decline in economic activity and a recession. Additionally, changes in consumer and business confidence can also lead to a recession. If consumers and businesses become less confident in the economy, they may reduce spending and investment, leading to a decline in economic activity.

Recessions can also be caused by external factors such as natural disasters, war, or changes in commodity prices. A natural disaster can disrupt production and supply chains, leading to a decline in economic activity. war can lead to a decline in trade and investment, and changes in commodity prices can lead to a decline in economic activity in countries that are heavily dependent on those commodities.

Governments can respond to recessions by implementing monetary policy, such as lowering interest rates, or fiscal policy, such as increasing government spending or cutting taxes. Lowering interest rates can make borrowing cheaper and encourage spending, while increasing government spending can provide a boost to demand. Cutting taxes can also put more money in people's pockets, leading to increased consumer spending. However, the effectiveness of these policies can vary and sometimes have unintended consequences.

It's important to note that recessions are a normal part of the business cycle and that economies typically recover from recessions over time.

However, the length and severity of a recession can vary depending on the underlying causes. Some recessions may be short and mild, while others can be long and severe. It's also important to note that not all countries or regions experience recessions at the same time, and the global economy can still grow during a recession in some countries.

Additionally, it's important to note that recessions have a disproportionate impact on certain groups, such as low-income families, small businesses, and minority communities. These groups may be more vulnerable to job losses, lower income, and reduced access to credit during a recession.

In conclusion, understanding economic recessions is crucial to understanding how the economy works and how to respond to them. It's important to be aware of the factors that can cause a recession and the impact it can have on society and the economy. Additionally, it's important to be aware of the policy tools available to governments to respond to recessions and the potential unintended consequences of those policies.

The Impact of Economic Recessions on Finances

Economic recessions can have a significant impact on an individual's finances. A recession is defined as a period of economic decline, typically characterized by a decrease in gross domestic product (GDP), an increase in unemployment, and a decline in the stock market.

During a recession, many individuals may lose their jobs or see their hours and wages reduced. This can lead to a decrease in income, making it harder for individuals to pay their bills and meet their financial obligations. As a result, many individuals may struggle to make ends meet and may be forced to dip into savings or take on additional debt.

In addition to a decrease in income, recessions can also lead to an increase in the cost of living. Prices for goods and services may rise, and the value of investments, such as stocks and real estate, may decrease. This can make it harder for individuals to maintain their standard of living and achieve their financial goals.

Recessions can also have a negative impact on the availability of credit. During a recession, banks and other lenders may become more cautious and may tighten lending standards. This can make it harder for individuals to obtain loans or credit, which can make it harder to purchase a home, start a business, or invest in other opportunities.

Furthermore, during a recession, the government may implement policies to stimulate economic growth, such as increasing government spending or lowering interest rates. While these policies can help to ease the effects of a recession, they can also have negative consequences, such as inflation or government debt.

Overall, economic recessions can have a significant impact on an individual's finances, affecting income, cost of living, access to credit, and the value of investments. It is important for individuals to be prepared for a recession by creating and maintaining a budget, saving for emergencies, and diversifying their investments. Being financially prepared for a recession will help to mitigate the negative impact it can have on an individual's finances.

CHAPTER TWO
Preparing for Economic Uncertainty

Preparing for economic uncertainty is an important step that individuals and families can take to protect their finances and ensure their long-term financial stability. Economic uncertainty can come in many forms, such as a recession, inflation, or a sudden change in government policies. Here are a few strategies that can help individuals prepare for economic uncertainty:

(a). Build an emergency fund: Having a savings account that you can rely on in case of job loss or other financial emergencies is essential. Try to keep at least three to six months' worth of expenses for living in an account that is simple to access.

(b). Diversify your investments: Diversifying your investment portfolio can help to spread risk and protect against market fluctuations. Take into account investing in a variety of stocks, bonds, properties, and other assets.

(c). Minimize debt: High levels of debt can make it harder to weather an economic downturn. Put paying off high-interest debt first, and refrain from taking on any further debt.

(d). Stay informed: Keep up-to-date with the latest economic news and trends. This will help you to anticipate potential changes in the market and adjust your financial plans accordingly.

(e). Make a budget and stick to it: A budget is a powerful tool that can help you to control your spending and ensure that you're saving enough money to meet your financial goals. Make periodically evaluate your budget and make any required modifications.

(f). Be flexible and adaptable: Economic uncertainty often means that plans and strategies will have to be adjusted to adapt to the changing circumstances. Be prepared to re-evaluate your financial plans and adjust them as necessary.

(g). Consider getting professional help: A financial advisor or a financial planner can be a great resource when it comes to navigating economic uncertainty. They can provide you with guidance on how to invest your money and develop a financial plan that is tailored to your specific needs and goals.

Preparing for economic uncertainty is an ongoing process that requires individuals and families to be proactive, informed, and adaptable. by following these strategies, you can protect your finances and ensure your long-term financial stability.

Building an Emergency Fund

An emergency fund is a savings account designated expressly for unforeseen costs or financial emergencies is known as an emergency fund. Building an emergency fund is an important step that individuals and families can take to protect their finances and ensure their long-term financial stability. There are a few key strategies for building an emergency fund.

The first step in building an emergency fund is to set a savings goal. a general rule of thumb is to aim for 3-6 months' worth of living expenses. This will provide enough cushion to cover expenses in case of a financial emergency such as job loss, unexpected medical bills, or major home repairs.

In the same fashion make a plan. Once you have set your savings goal, make a plan to achieve it. Break your goal down into smaller, more manageable steps and set a deadline for achieving each step.

Prioritize saving. Make saving for your emergency fund a priority. Set aside a specific amount of money each month, and consider setting up automatic transfers from your checking account to your savings account.

Cut expenses. To make room in your budget for saving, look for ways to cut expenses. Consider reducing your spending on discretionary items such as dining out, entertainment, or subscriptions you don't use.

Find extra income. Finding extra income can also help you to save more money for your emergency fund. Consider taking on a part-part-time job, starting a side hustle, or selling items you no longer need.

Keep the fund liquid. An emergency fund should be easily accessible when needed. Keep the fund in a liquid savings account, such as a high-yield savings account or a money market fund. Avoid keeping the fund in investments such as stocks, which can be hard to liquidate quickly in case of emergency.

Be patient. Building an emergency fund takes time and discipline, so be patient and stay committed to your plan. Remember, the goal is to have a cushion to fall back on in case of unexpected financial emergencies.

Finally, an emergency fund is a critical component of a solid financial plan. It provides a safety net to cover unexpected expenses and can help individuals and families to weather financial emergencies with less stress. Building an emergency fund takes time and discipline, but the peace of mind and financial security it provides is well worth the effort.

Assessing Your Financial Risk

Assessing your financial risk involves evaluating the likelihood that you will be able to meet your financial goals, given your current assets, liabilities, income, and expenses. To do this, you will need to gather information about your current financial situation, including your income, expenses, debts, and assets. You will also need to consider your future financial goals, such as saving for retirement or buying a home.

Once you have gathered this information, you can begin to assess your risk by looking at your debt-to-income ratio, which is the amount of debt you have compared to your income. A high ratio indicates that you may have difficulty making your debt payments, while a low ratio suggests that you have more disposable income to save or invest.

Another way to assess your risk is to look at your savings and investments. If you have a low amount of savings or investments, you may be at a higher risk of not being able to meet your financial goals. On the other hand, if you have a large amount of savings or investments, you may be in a better position to meet your financial goals.

It's also important to review your insurance coverage, such as life, health, and disability insurance to make sure that you have adequate coverage in case of unexpected events.

Overall, assessing your financial risk is a process that requires you to gather information about your current financial situation, consider your future financial goals, and evaluate your ability to meet those goals given your current assets and liabilities. once you have a good understanding of your financial risk, you can take steps to reduce that risk, such as by increasing your savings, paying down debt, or adjusting your investment strategy.

Developing a budget

Developing a budget during an economic recession can be a challenging task, as the downturn in the economy can lead to job loss, reduced income, and increased expenses. However, it is important to have a budget in place to manage your finances and make sure that you can meet your essential expenses.

The first step in developing a budget during a recession is to assess your current financial situation. This includes gathering information about your income, expenses, debts, and assets. You should also consider any potential changes to your income or expenses, such as job loss or reduced hours, and factor them into your budget.

Next, you should prioritize your expenses. During a recession, it is important to focus on essential expenses, such as housing, food, and healthcare, and reduce or eliminate non-essential expenses, such as entertainment or luxury items. You may also need to look for ways to reduce your expenses, such as negotiating with creditors or landlords for lower payments.

It's also important to have an emergency fund, which can help you to cover unexpected expenses or loss of income during the recession. If you don't have an emergency fund, you can start saving a small amount of money each month to build one.

Another key part of developing a budget during a recession is to look for ways to increase your income. This may include looking for a new job, taking on a part-time job, or starting a side business.

Finally, it's important to regularly review and adjust your budget as your financial situation changes during the recession. By staying on top of your finances and making adjustments as needed, you can help to ensure that you are able to meet your essential expenses and weather the economic downturn.

Overall, developing a budget during an economic recession requires careful assessment of your current financial situation, prioritizing expenses, having an emergency fund, and looking for ways to increase your income. By following these steps, you can help to manage your finances and make it through the recession.

CHAPTER THREE
Managing Debt

Managing debt during an economic recession can be a difficult task, as the downturn in the economy can lead to job loss, reduced income, and increased expenses. However, there are steps that you can take to manage your debt and stay on top of your finances during this challenging time.

The first step in managing debt during a recession is to assess your current financial situation. This includes gathering information about your income, expenses, debts, and assets. You should also consider any potential changes to your income or expenses, such as job loss or reduced hours, and factor them into your debt management plan.

Next, you should prioritize your debt payments. During a recession, it is important to focus on paying off high-interest debt, such as credit card balances, as these debts can quickly spiral out of control. You should also consider consolidating your debts into one loan with a lower interest rate, which can make it easier to manage your payments.

It's also important to communicate with your creditors and lenders during a recession, as they may be willing to work with you to modify your payment terms or offer temporary relief. If you have difficulty making your payments, you should reach out to your creditors as soon as possible to explain your situation.

Another key part of managing debt during a recession is to look for ways to increase your income. This may include looking for a new job, taking on a part-time job, or starting a side business. You can also look into governmental support programs that can help you to manage your debt during this time.

Finally, it's important to regularly review and adjust your debt management plan as your financial situation changes during the recession. By staying on top of your finances and making adjustments as needed, you can help to ensure that you are able to meet your debt payments and avoid falling behind on your loans.

Overall, managing debt during an economic recession requires careful assessment of your current financial situation, prioritizing debt payments, communicating with creditors, and looking for ways to increase your income. by following these steps, you can help to manage your debt and make it through the recession.

Strategies For Paying Off Debt

Paying off debt can be a challenging task, but there are several strategies that can help you to effectively manage and ultimately pay off your debts.

One popular strategy is the "debt snowball" method, which involves paying off your smallest debt first, while making the minimum payments on your larger debts. Once the smallest debt is paid off, you move on to the next smallest debt and so on, until all of your debts are paid off. The idea behind this method is that as you pay off each debt, you gain momentum and motivation to continue paying off your debts.

Another strategy is the "debt avalanche" method, which involves paying off your debt with the highest interest rate first, while making the minimum payments on your other debts. This strategy saves more money in the long run as the interest charges on high-interest debts can add up quickly.

Consolidation is another popular strategy. This involves combining multiple debts into one loan with a lower interest rate, making it easier to manage and pay off your debts. You can do this by taking out a personal loan, or by transferring high-interest credit card balances to a lower interest card.

You should also consider cutting unnecessary expenses and increasing your income, in order to make extra payments on your debt. This can be done by creating a budget, cutting back on luxuries, and finding ways to increase your income through side hustles or asking for a raise at work.

Finally, it's important to communicate with your creditors and lenders to discuss your financial situation and explore options such as modifying your payment terms or offering temporary relief.

Overall, paying off debt requires a combination of different strategies and a commitment to making regular payments. by prioritizing your debts, cutting unnecessary expenses and increasing your income, you can effectively manage and ultimately pay off your debts.

Navigating Credit Card Debt

Navigating credit card debt during an economic recession can be a difficult task, as the downturn in the economy can lead to job loss, reduced income, and increased expenses. However, there are steps that you can take to manage your credit card debt and stay on top of your finances during this challenging time.

The first step in managing credit card debt during a recession is to assess your current financial situation. This includes gathering information about your income, expenses, credit card balances, and available credit. you should also consider any potential changes to your income or expenses, such as job loss or reduced hours, and factor them into your debt management plan.

Next, you should prioritize your credit card payments. During a recession, it is important to focus on paying off high-interest credit card balances, as these debts can quickly spiral out of control. you should also consider consolidating your credit card debt into one loan with a lower interest rate, which can make it easier to manage your payments.

It's also important to communicate with your credit card companies and lenders during a recession, as they may be willing to work with you to modify your payment terms or offer temporary relief. If you have difficulty making your payments, you should reach out to your credit card companies as soon as possible to explain your situation.

Another key part of managing credit card debt during a recession is to look for ways to increase your income. This may include looking for a new job, taking on a part-time job, or starting a side business. You can also look into governmental support programs that can help you to manage your credit card debt during this time.

Finally, it's important to regularly review and adjust your credit card debt management plan as your financial situation changes during the recession. By staying on top of your finances and making adjustments as needed, you can help to ensure that you are able to meet your credit card payments and avoid falling behind on your balances.

Overall, managing credit card debt during an economic recession requires careful assessment of your current financial situation, prioritizing credit card payments, communicating with credit card companies and lenders, and looking for ways to increase your income. By following these steps, you can help to manage your credit card debt and make it through the recession.

Avoiding Predatory Lending

Predatory lending refers to the practice of lending money to individuals with high-risk credit or income, with the intention of taking advantage of their financial vulnerability. This type of lending can be particularly prevalent during economic recessions, as individuals may be more likely to turn to high-interest loans or credit products to make ends meet.

To avoid predatory lending during an economic recession, it's important to be aware of the warning signs of predatory lending practices. there are some key common indicators.
One of them is high-interest rates. predatory lenders often charge exorbitant interest rates, which can make it difficult for borrowers to repay their loans.

Predatory lenders may charge hidden fees, such as application fees or prepayment penalties, which can add to the overall cost of the loan.

Likewise, the pressure to borrow. predatory lenders may use high-pressure tactics to convince borrowers to take out a loan, even if they cannot afford it.

Predatory lenders may not fully disclose the terms and conditions of the loan, Making it difficult for borrowers to understand the true cost of the loan.

To avoid predatory lending, it's important to do your research before taking out a loan or credit product. This includes comparing rates and terms from different lenders, as well as reading the fine print to understand the full cost of the loan. you can also use online resources like the consumer financial protection bureau (CFPB) or national foundation for credit counseling (NFCC) to find reputable lenders and credit counseling services.

Additionally, you should be cautious of online lenders, especially those that don't have physical branches and offer easy loans without proper credit check.

It's also important to think carefully about whether you actually need the loan, and if so, whether you can afford to repay it. If you're struggling to make ends meet, it may be better to seek out government assistance or credit counseling instead of taking out a high-interest loan.

Finally, if you suspect that you have been a victim of predatory lending, you should report it to the proper authorities, such as the CFPB or the federal trade commission (FTC).

In conclusion, avoiding predatory lending during an economic recession requires being aware of the warning signs, researching different loan options and lenders, thinking carefully about whether you need the loan, and reporting any suspected predatory lending activities.

CHAPTER FOUR
Investing In A Volatile Economy

Investing in a volatile economy during a recession can be a challenging task, as economic uncertainty and market fluctuations can make it difficult to predict the performance of various assets. However, there are still opportunities to be found for investors who are willing to do their research and take a long-term perspective.

One strategy for investing in a volatile economy is to diversify your portfolio by including a mix of different asset classes, such as stocks, bonds, real estate, and precious metals. This can help to spread out your risk and reduce the impact of any one investment performing poorly.

Another strategy is to focus on investing in companies that have strong fundamentals and are likely to weather the economic downturn. These may include companies with strong balance sheets, solid cash flow, and a history of profitability. Additionally, investors may want to look for companies that are well-positioned to benefit from long-term trends, such as the growth of e-commerce or the shift towards renewable energy.

It's also important to keep in mind that investing in a volatile economy during a recession can be a long-term play and it is essential to have a long-term perspective. While there may be short-term dips and setbacks, over time, the markets will recover and many investors will be able to earn attractive returns.

It's also worth noting that, during a recession, many investors tend to move away from riskier investments, such as stocks, and move more into safer investments, such as bonds. this leads to a decrease in stock prices, and often leads to buying opportunities for investors with a long-term perspective.

In summary, investing in a volatile economy during a recession requires a mix of both patience and research. by diversifying your portfolio, focusing on companies with strong fundamentals, and having a long-term perspective, investors can still find opportunities for growth despite the uncertainty of the economy.

Identifying Safe Investments

Identifying safe investments during an economic recession can be a challenge, as market fluctuations and uncertainty can make it difficult to predict the performance of various assets. However, there are certain investment options that tend to be less risky and can provide a level of stability in a volatile economy.

One safe investment option during a recession is government bonds. These are debt securities issued by the government and are considered to be among the safest investments because they are backed by the full faith and credit of the government. this means that the government is obliged to pay the bondholder the face value of the bond at maturity, and to pay periodic interest on the bond until maturity.

Another safe investment option is cash and cash equivalents, such as savings accounts and money market funds. these investments are considered to be safe because they have low risk of loss of principal and are easily liquidated.

Certificates of deposit (CDs) are another safe investment option during a recession. cds are savings certificates with a fixed term and fixed interest rate, issued by banks and other financial institutions. CDs are FDIC-insured, meaning that they are backed by the full faith and credit of the government and are considered to be a safe place to park your money during a recession.

Investing in real estate can also be a safe option during a recession, as long as the property is in a stable or improving market, and is purchased at a reasonable price. real estate can provide a steady stream of rental income and can appreciate in value over time, which can be a hedge against inflation.

During a recession, it's important to focus on safe investments that have low risk of loss of principal and are easily liquidated. government bonds, cash and cash equivalents, CDs, and real estate can be considered as safe investment options during a recession. However, it's important to understand that no investment is completely risk-free and investors should always do their own research and consult a financial advisor before making any investment decisions.

Understanding Market Cycles

Understanding market cycles is important for investors in order to make informed decisions during an economic recession. A market cycle is the natural up and down movement of the economy and financial markets, characterized by periods of expansion and contraction.

The business cycle or market cycle is the natural fluctuation of economic activity that includes periods of economic growth and expansion, followed by periods of contraction and recession. The most commonly recognized stages of the business cycle are expansion, peak, contraction, and trough.

During an expansion, the economy is growing and financial markets are generally performing well. This is typically characterized by low unemployment, rising wages, and increasing consumer and business confidence. as a result, stocks tend to rise and bond yields tend to fall.

As the economy reaches a peak, growth starts to slow and the risk of a recession increases. At this stage, investors should be cautious and focus on identifying safe investments.

During a contraction or recession, the economy is in a downturn and financial markets are generally performing poorly. This is characterized by rising unemployment, falling wages, and decreasing consumer and business confidence. As a result, stocks tend to fall and bond yields tend to rise.

The trough is the final stage of the contraction, marking the end of the recession and the start of a new expansion. This is characterized by a rebound in economic activity and financial markets.

It's important to note that market cycles are not regular or predictable, and can vary in length and severity. However, understanding the stages of the market cycle can help investors make more informed decisions during an economic recession, such as identifying safe investments and having a long-term perspective.

In summary, understanding market cycles is crucial for investors to make informed decisions during an economic recession. the market cycle is the natural up and down movement of the economy and financial markets characterized by periods of expansion and contraction. recognizing the stages of the market cycle can help investors identify safe investments and have a long-term perspective.

Diversifying Your Investment Portfolio

Diversifying your investment portfolio is important in any

economic environment, but it becomes even more critical during a recession. Diversification is the practice of spreading your investments across different asset classes, sectors, and geographic regions, in order to spread risk and minimize the impact of any one investment on your overall portfolio.

One way to diversify your portfolio during a recession is to invest in multiple asset classes, such as stocks, bonds, and cash. this can provide a balance of growth and income, as well as a level of safety and liquidity.

Another way to diversify your portfolio is to invest in different sectors, such as technology, healthcare, and consumer goods. This can provide a balance of risk and return, as well as a hedge against market fluctuations in any one sector.

You can also diversify your portfolio by investing in different geographic regions, such as the United States, Europe, and Asia. This can provide a balance of risk and return, as well as a hedge against economic fluctuations in any one region.

Another strategy to consider is investing in alternative investments such as real estate, private equity, or hedge funds. These types of investments can provide a level of diversification, as they tend to have low correlation to the stock market, which can provide a hedge against market volatility.

In summary, diversifying your investment portfolio is crucial during a recession, as it can help spread risk and minimize the impact of any one investment on your overall portfolio. This can be achieved by investing in multiple asset classes, sectors, and geographic regions, as well as exploring alternative investments. It's important to remember that diversification does not guarantee a profit or protect against loss, but it can help manage risk by spreading it across different types of investments.

CHAPTER FIVE
Protecting Your Career and Income

Protecting your career and income during an economic recession is essential to ensure that you are able to maintain your standard of living and continue to support yourself and your family. A few strategies to think about are listed below:

Be proactive. Anticipate potential challenges and opportunities in your industry and take steps to prepare for them. This may include developing new skills, building a professional network, or seeking out new job opportunities.

Diversify your income. Consider taking on a part-time job, freelancing, or starting a side business to supplement your primary income. This can provide a safety net in case of job loss or reduction in hours.

Build an emergency fund. Having a savings cushion can help you weather a job loss or reduction in income. aim to have at least six months' worth of living expenses saved up in case of emergency.

Network. Building and maintaining strong professional connections can help you stay informed about job opportunities and industry trends. It can also help you make valuable connections that can support you in your career.

Keep your skills relevant. Invest in your professional development by taking courses, attending seminars, or pursuing further education. This can increase your chances of finding employment or staying competitive in your current role.

Be aware of government aid. Keep an eye out for any government aid programs that may be available to help you through difficult times.

Be open to change. Be prepared to adjust your career goals or explore alternative career paths if necessary. This may include taking on temporary or part-time work, or starting your own business.

In conclusion, protecting your career and income during an economic recession requires being proactive, diversifying your income, building an emergency fund, networking, keeping your skills relevant, being aware of government aid and being open to change. While it's important to be strategic and take steps to mitigate risk, it's also important to remain optimistic and stay open to new opportunities that may arise during difficult times.

Identifying Job Loss Risks

During an economic recession, job loss can become a reality for many individuals and families. Identifying the signs that your job may be at risk can help you prepare and take steps to mitigate the impact.

Company financials. Look for signs of financial distress such as decreased revenue, layoffs, or the closure of branches or subsidiaries.

Changes in the company. Be aware of changes in the company's direction or focus, such as a shift in priorities or a change in leadership.

Your own job performance. If your job performance has been slipping, or you are not meeting expectations, it may put you at risk for being let go.

Company's hiring/recruiting. If the company is not hiring or recruiting, it could be a sign that they are trying to cut costs by not replacing employees who leave.

Company's downsizing. If the company is downsizing and reducing the number of employees, it could put your job at risk.

Company's outsourcing. if the company is outsourcing jobs to other countries, it may lead to job loss for employees in the affected positions.

Company's automation. If the company is automating jobs, it may lead to job loss for employees in the affected positions.

It's important to note that job loss is a possibility during an economic recession and it's crucial to prepare for it, by being aware of the above signs, keeping an eye out for alternative job opportunities, keeping your skills relevant, and building an emergency fund.

Identifying job loss in an economic recession is crucial to prepare for it. Some of the signs to look for are a company's financials, changes in the company, job performance, hiring/recruiting, downsizing, outsourcing, and automation.

Building a Strong Professional Network

Building a strong professional network is important in any economic climate, but it becomes even more crucial during an economic recession. Having a robust network of contacts in your industry can help you stay informed about job opportunities, industry trends, and potential challenges. here are a few strategies to consider when building a professional network:

Attend industry events. Attend conferences, seminars, and networking events related to your industry. this will allow you to meet other professionals in your field and learn about the latest trends and developments.

Join professional organizations. Joining professional organizations in your industry can provide you with access to valuable resources, events, and networking opportunities.

Connect on LinkedIn. Linkedin is a great platform to connect with professionals in your industry. join groups, participate in discussions, and make connections with people in your field.

 Keep in touch with former colleagues and classmates. Maintaining connections with former colleagues and classmates can be a valuable resource in your professional network. reach out to them periodically to stay in touch and let them know about your current career goals.

Collaborate with others. Collaborating with other professionals in your field on projects, research, or publications can help you build relationships and establish yourself as an expert in your field.

Be helpful and supportive. Building a professional network is not just about what you can gain, but also about what you can give. be helpful and supportive of others in your network, and they will be more likely to return the favor.

Volunteer. Give back to your community by volunteering for organizations and causes that align with your interests and career goals.

it can be a fantastic opportunity to meet new people and develop meaningful relationships.

Building a strong professional network in an economic recession is crucial to stay informed about job opportunities, industry trends, and potential challenges. some strategies to consider are attending industry events, joining professional organizations, connecting on linkedin, keeping in touch with former colleagues and classmates, collaborating with others, being helpful and supportive, and volunteering.

Strategies For Job Searching in a Downturn

Job searching during an economic downturn can be challenging, but there are strategies you can use to increase your chances of finding a job.

Update your resume and online profiles. make sure your resume and online profiles are up-to-date, and highlight the skills and experiences that are most relevant to the jobs you are applying for.

Network. Reach out to people in your professional network, including former colleagues and classmates, to see if they know of any job openings. to grow your network, go to networking events and join groups for professionals.

Be flexible. Consider taking a temporary or contract job, or accepting a role that is not exactly what you are looking for, as a way to gain experience and earn income while you continue to search for a permanent job.

Be open to remote jobs. Wih the pandemic, more companies are open to hiring remote workers, so consider remote jobs as an option

Use online job search platforms. Utilize online job search platforms such as linkedin, indeed, and glassdoor to find job openings that match your skills and experience.

Tailor your resume to the job. When applying for a job, tailor your resume and cover letter to match the requirements listed in the job description.

Be proactive. Apply for jobs before they are posted. reach out to companies you are interested in working for and express your interest in the company and any open positions.

Be persistent. Job searching can be a long process, and it's important to stay persistent and keep trying. Don't get discouraged if you don't hear back from a company or if you don't get the job.

Job searching during an economic downturn can be challenging but there are strategies you can use to increase your chances of finding a job. Some strategies include updating your resume and online profiles, networking, being flexible, being open to remote jobs, using online job search platforms, tailoring your resume to the job, being proactive, and being persistent.

CHAPTER SIX
Supporting Your Community

Supporting your community during an economic recession is important for maintaining its well-being. you can assist in the following ways:

Volunteer your time. Offer your services to local non-profit organizations or charities that support those in need.

Shop locally. Spend your money at small, local businesses to help keep them afloat.

Donate to food banks. Food insecurity can increase during economic downturns, consider making a financial or food donation to your local food bank.

Support the arts. Attend local concerts, theater productions, or art exhibitions to show support for the creative

Help with job search. Offer your skills, network or mentorship to help someone in your community find employment.

Advocate for policy change. Write to your elected officials and advocate for policies that support families and individuals during tough economic times.

Remember, small actions can have a big impact on the health and well-being of your community during an economic recession.

The Role of Government in Economic Recessions

The role of government in economic recessions is critical for maintaining stability and supporting citizens and businesses. Here are some ways government can play a role:

Stimulate the economy. Governments can provide fiscal stimulus through tax cuts, increased spending, or infrastructure projects to boost economic activity.

Provide financial support. Governments can offer financial support to individuals and businesses through programs such as unemployment insurance, small business loans, and mortgage forbearance.

Regulate the financial sector. Governments can implement regulations to prevent excessive risk-taking by financial institutions and prevent the spread of economic instability.

Invest in education and training. Governments can invest in education and training programs to help individuals acquire new skills and increase their employability during a recession.

Maintain stability. Governments can take actions to maintain stability in financial markets and prevent panic through measures such as providing guarantees for bank deposits.

Promote international cooperation. Governments can work together with other countries to coordinate responses to global economic challenges and promote stability.

The role of government in an economic recession is vital for promoting stability, supporting citizens and businesses, and laying the foundation for long-term economic growth. A strong and effective government response can help mitigate the impact of an economic downturn and ensure a quicker recovery.

Supporting Local Businesses

Supporting local businesses during an economic recession is important for maintaining the health and vitality of your community. you can assist in the following ways:

Shop locally. Choose to spend your money at small, local businesses instead of large corporations.

Spread the word. Share your positive experiences with friends and family and recommend local businesses to others.

Write positive online reviews. leave a positive review for local businesses on websites such as yelp or tripadvisor to help attract new customers.

Buy gifts from local shops. Consider buying gifts for birthdays, holidays, or other special occasions from local businesses.

Participate in local events. Attend local events and festivals, which can help drive foot traffic to local businesses.

Order takeout or delivery from local restaurants. Help support local restaurants by ordering takeout or delivery instead of dining in.

Remember, supporting local businesses during an economic recession is a small but powerful way to help ensure their long-term success and vitality. By showing your support, you can help create a stronger and more resilient community.

Volunteering and Philanthropy

The role of government in economic recessions is critical for maintaining stability and supporting citizens and businesses. here are some ways government can play a role:

Stimulate the economy. Governments can provide fiscal stimulus through tax cuts, increased spending, or infrastructure projects to boost economic activity.

Provide financial support. Governments can offer financial support to individuals and businesses through programs such as unemployment insurance, small business loans, and mortgage forbearance.

Regulate the financial sector. Governments can implement regulations to prevent excessive risk-taking by financial institutions and prevent the spread of economic instability.

Promote international cooperation. governments can work together with other countries to coordinate responses to global economic challenges and promote stability.

In conclusion, the role of government in an economic recession is vital for promoting stability, supporting citizens and businesses, and laying the foundation for long-term economic growth. A strong and effective government response can help mitigate the impact of an economic downturn and ensure a quicker recovery.

CHAPTER SEVEN
Staying resilient in times of uncertainty

Staying resilient during times of economic uncertainty can be challenging, but it is important for maintaining mental and emotional well-being. Here are some tips for staying resilient:

Take care of your physical health. Exercise regularly, eat a balanced diet, and get plenty of rest.

Maintain a support system. Stay connected with friends, family, and community members who provide support and encouragement.

Practice gratitude. Take time each day to reflect on what you are thankful for and focus on the positive aspects of your life.

Set achievable goals. focus on setting and achieving small, manageable goals to maintain a sense of control and purpose.

Engage in activities you enjoy. pursue hobbies, interests, and other activities that bring you joy and a sense of accomplishment.

Seek professional help. if necessary, seek the assistance of a mental health professional to help you manage stress and anxiety.

In conclusion, staying resilient during an economic recession requires a combination of self-care and support from others. by focusing on your physical and emotional well-being and seeking help when needed, you can navigate uncertainty with confidence and resilience.

CONCLUSION

After an economic recession, it is important for individuals, businesses and governments to focus on moving forward and rebuilding their economies. Here are some key steps to consider:

Prioritize stability. Establishing financial stability is crucial in order to move forward after a recession. This includes reducing debt and creating a solid plan for future spending.

Invest in education and training. Investing in education and training can help individuals acquire new skills and increase their competitiveness in the job market.

Foster entrepreneurship. Encouraging entrepreneurship and small business growth can create jobs and stimulate economic growth.

Promote economic diversification. Relying too heavily on one industry can lead to economic vulnerability. Encouraging a diverse range of industries can mitigate this risk. Strengthen social safety nets. A strong safety net can help protect vulnerable individuals during economic downturns and provide a foundation for recovery.

Promote international trade. International trade can provide new markets for goods and services, creating new opportunities for growth.

Invest in infrastructure. Investing in infrastructure such as transportation and communication systems can improve efficiency and competitiveness.

Overall, the key to moving forward after an economic recession is to focus on stability, growth and resilience. This requires a combination of short-term actions and long-term planning, as well as cooperation between individuals, businesses, and governments.